The Fabian Society

The Fabian Society is Britain's lead... political society, committed to creati... debates which can shape the future o...

With over 300 Fabian MPs, MEPs, Peers, ... plays an unparalleled role in linking the ... debates at the highest level with vigorous ... growing membership of over 7000 people, ... regularly throughout Britain and a vibrant Y... organising its own activities. Fabian publicati... therefore reach and influence a wider audien... those of any comparable think tank. The Society is unique among think tanks in being a thriving, democratically-constituted membership organisation, affiliated to the Labour Party but organisationally and editorially independent.

For over 120 years Fabians have been central to every important renewal and revision of left of centre thinking. The Fabian commitment to open and participatory debate is as important today as ever before as we explore the ideas, politics and policies which will define the next generation of progressive politics in Britain, Europe and around the world. Find out more at **www.fabians.org.uk**

The TUC

The TUC is the voice of Britain at work. With 66 affiliated unions representing nearly seven million working people from all walks of life, we campaign for a fair deal at work and for social justice at home and abroad. The TUC negotiates in Europe and at home, building links with political parties, business, local communities and wider society. For more information, go to **www.tuc.org.uk**

Fabian Society
11 Dartmouth Street
London SW1H 9BN
www.fabians.org.uk

Fabian ideas
Editorial Director: Tom Hampson
Pamphlet editor: Hannah Jameson

First published 2008

ISBN 978 0 7163 06238
ISSN 1746-1146

British Library Cataloguing in Publication data.
A catalogue record for this book is available from the British Library.

How to Defend Inheritance Tax

by Rajiv Prabhakar, Karen Rowlingson
and Stuart White

FABIAN SOCIETY

In asssociation with

TUC

About the authors

Rajiv Prabhakar is a lecturer in the organisation and delivery of health services at the London School of Hygiene and Tropical Medicine. He is the author of Stakeholding and New Labour (2003) and Rethinking Public Services (2006). His latest book is The Assets Agenda (Palgrave MacMillan, 2008).

Karen Rowlingson is a Professor of Social Policy at the University of Birmingham. Her current research interests lie in the financial security of individuals, families and households including: assets and asset-based welfare; poverty, wealth and inequality; social security policy; and financial planning and management (including savings, pensions, credit and debt). She has recently completed a study of attitudes to inequality (with Michael Orton) and attitudes to inheritance (with Stephen McKay).

Stuart White teaches political theory at Jesus College, and is Director of the Public Policy Unit in the Department of Politics and International Relations, Oxford University. His research focuses on egalitarianism in theory and practice with a particular interest in exploring political theories which are critical both of capitalism and statism, and policy ideas related to these currents of thought. He is the editor of New Labour: The Progressive Future? (2001), the author of The Civic Minimum (2003) and Equality (2006), and co-editor, with Will Paxton and Dominic Maxwell, of The Citizen's Stake (2006) and, with Daniel Leighton, of the forthcoming volume, Building a Citizen Society.

Acknowledgments

The authors would like to thank the participants at a seminar on 'The Ethics and Politics of Inheritance Tax', hosted by the Public Policy Unit at Oxford University on September 28 2007, at which many of the themes of this pamphlet were first aired.

Particular thanks to Tom Hampson, Tim Horton and Hannah Jameson at the Fabian Society for their interest in and support for the project, and to the following for their thoughts on the topic: Matthew Clayton, John Cunliffe, Keith Dowding, Barbara Fried, Martin O'Neill, Michael Otsuka, Andrew Reeve, Jonathan Riley, Hillel Steiner, Polly Toynbee, Karl Widerquist, and Andrew Williams. We, of course, remain responsible for any errors. Rajiv Prabhakar would also like gratefully to acknowledge the financial assistance received from the Economic and Social Research Council for the project The Assets Agenda: principles and policy (RES 000-27-0164) which helped fund his work on inheritance tax.

The authors wish to thank the editors of the *Political Quarterly* and Blackwell publishers for permission to publish some material which is also due to appear in a symposium on inheritance tax in a forthcoming issue of the journal. We would like to thank the Andrew Wainwright Reform Trust for their support of this project and the TUC without whose involvement this publication would not have been possible.

Karen Rowlingson would like to thank the Joseph Rowntree Foundation for their financial support for the work on attitudes on inheritance on which we draw here, and Stephen McKay for his contribution to that work.

Stuart White would like to dedicate this pamphlet in memory of Andrew Glyn, a great teacher, scholar and egalitarian.

Last, but certainly not least, we would all like to warmly thank our families for their support.

Comments on 'How to Defend Inheritance Tax'

The race by politicians to cut a tax paid only by the wealthiest one in twenty estates shows just how progressives have failed to make the case for a fair tax system in recent years. It is time to spell out that cuts in tax for the wealthy mean either higher taxes for everyone else or poorer public services. This pamphlet is a valuable contribution to the fightback.
– Brendan Barber, TUC General Secretary

The treatment of inherited wealth was the 'tax bombshell" of 2007. It derailed the government's political strategy and offered the Conservative Party a populist device to reopen the argument about the taxation of aspiration. It is very welcome then that Stuart White and his colleagues have developed a vigorous defence of Inheritance tax. They demolish the Conservative case with elegant, relentless and merciless logic, advance a positive agenda for reform and develop practical proposals to build a winning political coalition.

This is an important pamphlet. Measured in argument and intellectually self-confident, it should be required reading for all those committed to an equalisation of life chances and a fairer distribution of income.
– David Coats, Deputy Director, the Work Foundation

This is a great pamphlet – smart, savvy, timely and very well-informed. Building public support for fair taxation lies at the heart of a new progressive agenda dedicated to justice and equality.
– Michael Edwards, Director, Governance and Civil Society, the Ford Foundation

This important and cogently argued study should be read by all those who believe – or say they believe – in greater equality of opportunity and in a fair system of taxation.
– John Hills, Centre for Analyis of Social Exclusion, London School of Economics

This is a brilliant and overdue exposition. I read it with profit and pleasure, and recommend it as a core text not just for Fabian members but for anybody interested in how our taxation system should be organised.
– Will Hutton, Director, the Work Foundation

All progressives (and indeed non-progressives) should read this – especially if, as sadly too many are, they are tempted to try to avoid what the authors convincingly demonstrate is one of the fairest of all taxes.
– Julian Le Grand, Richard Titmuss Professor of Social Policy at the London School of Economics

This Fabian pamphlet on inheritance tax opens up a key debate for social democrats: in a society that needs both more enterprise and greater fairness, where do we strike the balance between a natural parental desire to do their best for their children and how much the better off should be able to pass on in gifts without the children having to work hard to succeed on their own account. And how might we use a reformed inheritance tax to promote the channeling of a greater portion of the top 1 per cent's greatly increased share of national income and wealth into widening life chances for the most deprived.
– Roger Liddle, Vice Chair, Policy Network

At last, the moral case for inheritance tax is made clearly, convincingly and succinctly in this much needed pamphlet. At a time when the wealth and income gap is undermining equal life chances and our common citizenship, we badly need an informed debate on the role that a reformed inheritance tax can play in building a more just society. Armed with this ammunition, I hope the Fabian Society will now spearhead the 'citizen led' campaign for fair taxation for which the authors call.
– Ruth Lister, Professor of Social Policy, Loughborough University

I warmly welcome this important contribution to the debate about inheritance tax. The Labour Government has reformed the tax, benefiting the most prosperous children in the UK, seemingly as a response to a prolonged but desperately misleading media campaign. There has been too much nonsense written about 'double taxation'. The arguments put forward in this pamphlet expose that for the nonsense it is.

Inheritance Tax or a reformed version of it – set at a reasonable level as outlined in the Fabian Society pamphlet – is one way of mitigating against the increasing concentration of wealth and opportunity.

Rather than easing the so called 'burden' of inheritance tax, which affects only about 6 per cent of the population, the Government might have invested in the 3.8million children locked in poverty in the UK. It is those children who will pay for the Government's largesse.
– Martin Narey, Chief Executive, Barnardo's

Contents

“

Introduction

Why was there no general election in 2007?

Almost certainly the answer can be summarised in two words: inheritance tax. On the Friday after the Labour Party's annual conference, the expectation was that Gordon Brown would announce a general election at some point in the following two weeks. But the following Monday, at the Conservative Party conference, Shadow Chancellor George Osborne signalled the 'death knell for the death tax' with his promise to raise the inheritance tax threshold from £300,000 to £1 million. The proposal revived the popularity of the Conservative Party, particularly in key marginal seats, and put an end to talk of an October or November election. The Conservative proposal did not come out of the blue. It emerged against the background of a long-standing media campaign against inheritance tax taking in papers like the *Daily Express*, the *Daily Mail* and, not least, the Richard and Judy Show. In the wake of Osborne's announcement, even the allegedly liberal *Observer* chose to renew its campaign to 'reform' (that is to say, cut) inheritance tax, offering fresh advice to its progressive, liberal-minded readership on how to avoid it.

The reaction of the Labour government to the Osborne proposals is instructive. The Chancellor Alistair Darling used his 2007 pre-budget report and comprehensive spending review to announce that Labour would raise the thresholds for married couples and civil partners immediately to £600,000, rising to £700,000 in 2010-2011 (Her Majesty's Treasury 2007). Having made little or no effort to defend the tax robustly in the preceding few years, Labour was pushed onto the defensive, unable at short-notice to challenge the arguments against the tax and the misconceptions which underpin them. Debate about the taxation of inheritance – or, more generally, the transmission of wealth across the generations – need not and should not be conducted in this way. There are very strong arguments for inheritance tax. At the same time, the arguments made by the critics of inheritance tax are much weaker than they suppose.

First, some form of inheritance tax is essential if the tax system as a whole is to be fair. It is patently unfair to tax earnings from hard work while leaving unearned inheritances and gifts, which often reflect nothing more than accident of birth, untaxed. Second, inequality in financial inheritances contributes to overall inequality of opportunity. In combination with other policies, inheritance tax is essential to combat this source of unequal opportunity. A concern for equal opportunity, or 'equal life chances', is reflected in government commitments to end child poverty and to narrow the attainment gap between social classes in higher education. But the government's recent move to raise the threshold for inheritance tax is inconsistent with this commitment. Politicians and commentators across the political spectrum frequently wax lyrical about the virtues of equal opportunity and the related idea of 'meritocracy'. But without a commitment to equalize financial inheritances, these warm words lack credibility. On the other hand, inheritance tax is not necessarily a 'double tax', as the critics claim. Nor is it clear why it would matter if it was. Inheritance tax does not, on balance, necessarily penalize or discourage 'virtuous' behaviour, or have a significant negative effect on work and saving.

Our aim, then, is to add to the effort to stimulate a fresh and deeper public debate over inheritance tax. We wish to promote a real debate, a debate in which there are actually two sides, rather than one which consists almost entirely of critics loudly carping at a government which responds with little more than a twitchy silence. We are under no illusions as to the unpopularity of inheritance tax or of the difficulty of shifting public opinion even when people are exposed to relevant information and argument (Lewis and White 2006). But as the events of 2007 have shown, there is no longer any mileage for supporters of inheritance tax in just trying to keep quiet about the issue in the hope that it won't make it onto the political agenda. The opponents have now put it there. The only feasible response is to engage at the level of ideas by putting the positive case for inheritance tax. Moreover, a careful study of public opinion, and of the lessons to be learned from the repeal of the estate tax in the United States, can help us see how such a case might get public support.

1 | What is Inheritance Tax?

Let's start by clarifying what we mean by inheritance tax. In this pamphlet, unless otherwise indicated, we use the term 'inheritance tax' as a convenient shorthand to denote *any tax mechanism which seeks to tax wealth transfers across the generations (including but not necessarily only at death).*

So defined, inheritance tax takes a variety of forms. One issue concerns whether the tax falls on the estate of the deceased or on the amount received by the recipient of the wealth transfer. The former is an *estate tax,* and the tax liability will typically rise with the size of the estate. In the latter case, the tax depends on the amount a person inherits (which might only be a portion of a donor's whole estate). Strictly speaking, it is this sort of tax which is properly called an *inheritance tax.*

A second issue is what is included in the tax. One approach is only to tax transfers of wealth at death. A broader approach is to extend this and include the gifts that one person receives from another living person. A *capital receipts tax* covers both gifts and inheritances.

A third issue concerns the time period over which a tax is levied. A tax could be set upon all the gifts and inheritances that a person receives over their lifetime. This is a *lifetime capital receipts tax*. Alternatively, one might impose such a tax at regular intervals, for example annually. With any of the above taxes, one also has to set the appropriate threshold(s) and rate(s).

It is important throughout to remember that there are a variety of forms that inheritance taxation might take, and we shall refer to the different kinds of tax in the course of discussion and when discussing reform options in Chapter 5.

Inheritance tax in the United Kingdom

From the way the press talks about inheritance tax hitting or threatening 'middle England', one might think that the tax falls on a majority, or at least a large minority, of estates. In fact, at present only a small minority of estates pay inheritance tax. Her Majesty's Revenue and Customs (2007) reports that in 2004-05 there were around 583,000 deaths in the United Kingdom and about 5.4 per cent of all estates paid the tax.

The present UK inheritance tax was introduced in 1986. Strictly speaking, this is a form of estate tax as it is levied upon a donor's estate. As of 2006-07, the first £285,000 of a person's estate was exempt from any taxation. Anything above this £285,000 threshold was liable for a 40 per cent tax. There are various exemptions, however, above these thresholds. For example, under certain conditions agricultural property and business assets are free from the tax.[1] These exemptions are one factor explaining how it is possible largely to avoid the tax with the appropriate legal and financial advice. As noted, following the government's changes to the tax announced in October 2007, the threshold at which tax becomes payable will effectively rise to £600,000 for married couples and those in civil partnerships.

As Table 1.1 shows, receipts of inheritance tax have increased in the past three years. One likely reason is that the numbers paying this tax has increased. For example, Her Majesty's Revenue and Customs reports that the estimated numbers of those paying taxes on transfers at death rose from 29,000 in 2003-04 to 33,000 in 2006-07 (22,000 paid in 2000-01).[2] Nevertheless, as noted, this still represents only just over 5 per cent of estates.

Table 1.1 Inheritance tax receipts, 2000/01-2006/07

	Year						
IHT receipts £ billion	2000-01	2001-02	2002-03	2003-04	2004-05	2005-06	2006-07
	2.2	2.4	2.4	2.5	2.9	3.3	3.5

Adapted from: Her Majesty's Revenue and Customs, table 12.1, at http://www.hmrc.gov.uk/stats/inheritance_tax/table12-1.pdf. 1 billion = 1,000 million.

Inheritance tax only forms a small part of the total tax raised by government. In 2006-07, for example, inheritance tax represented only 0.8 per cent of the total tax yield (for comparison, income tax and value added tax comprised 34 per cent and 18 per cent respectively).[3] However, it is important not to underestimate the importance of this revenue stream. There are a lot of good things that can be done with £3.5 billion, such as financing policies which spread asset ownership to the population at large. In addition, we must recall that the present inheritance tax not only affects a small minority of estates but, related to this, absorbs only a small percentage of the total amount of wealth transferred at death. If the tax system was more effective at taxing wealth transfers, such taxes could account for a larger share of total tax revenue (though such taxes are obviously unlikely ever to compete with income tax as revenue raisers).

Public opinion

From the press one would also get the impression that people do not like inheritance tax. In this case, the perception one has looking at the press is closer to the truth. There have been several recent studies in Britain of public attitudes towards inheritance tax. A common theme of these studies is the unpopularity of this tax.

Alan Hedges and Catherine Bromley (2001) conducted a quantitative survey of public attitudes to taxation for the Fabian Society Commission on Taxation and Citizenship. This covered 1,717 adults in the summer of 2000. They found that 51 per cent of respondents thought that inheritance tax should be abolished, while around 20 per cent thought that the threshold at which inheritance tax starts should be raised from its then level of £250,000 to at least £500,000. The remainder believed that the current level should be kept or reduced, with a mere 2 per cent thinking that all inheritances should be taxed. This research suggested that younger people are more opposed to inheritance tax than older people, and that lower income individuals are more hostile than those on higher incomes.

What drives this opposition? Work undertaken with focus groups by Lewis and White (2006) and Prabhakar (2008a, 2008b) points to a mix of concerns. On the one hand, there are concerns about the perceived unfairness of the tax. In particular, there is a widespread view that inheritance tax is unfair because it is a 'double tax'. People argue that they have paid tax once on the income out of which they have accumulated their assets and so it is unfair to then place a further tax on these assets when they are transferred at death. On the other hand, there are concerns related to rising house prices. People are worried that house price inflation means that increasing numbers of ordinary families will find themselves liable for this tax. These fears are not confined to those who live in south-east England.

Restarting the debate

The public debate over inheritance tax has thus far been a rather one-sided debate – if the word 'debate' is appropriate at all. The critics have levelled their objections across a wide range of media outlets. The defence of inheritance tax has been relatively muted. It is, however, unfair just to blame the government for this. It is not as if politicians bear sole responsibility for challenging the case against inheritance tax. The campaign against the tax was pioneered in no small part by citizen activists. So should be the campaign in its defence. This pamphlet aims to explore the arguments of the critics, and the responses that will support citizen activists to lead this debate.

However, in order to restart the debate there are two key things we need to do.

First, we need to take stock of the relevant factual information and the moral arguments to see whether and why there is, in fact, a strong case for inheritance tax. To this end, Chapter 2 outlines data on the current spread of inheritances and reviews the literature on the significance of inherited wealth for inequality. Chapter 3 clarifies the main moral arguments for inheritance tax. Chapter 4 outlines and responds to common objections to inheritance tax, including the widespread double tax objection.

Second, we need to draw lessons where we can for political strategy and think about reform options which fit with this strategy. To this end, Chapter 5 takes another look at public opinion work from the UK and also at what we can learn from the repeal of the estate tax in the United States. From these sources, it identifies some basic principles of political strategy. Finally, it uses these principles to identify some possible progressive lines of reform of inheritance tax.

2 | Inheritance and Inequality

The growth of owner-occupation in the 1980s, particularly through the 'Right to Buy' scheme, led Nigel Lawson, the Chancellor of the Exchequer at the time, to claim that Britain was 'about to become a nation of inheritors'. His view was that this would spread wealth more evenly throughout the population. However, the gap between rich and poor actually began to rise in the 1990s for the first time that century. For example, the top 1 per cent of the population increased its share of personal wealth from 17 per cent to 23 per cent between 1988 and 1999 (Paxton 2002). And the Gini coefficient, a statistical measure of inequality, rose from 64 per cent to 70 per cent between 1991 and 2001 (Inland Revenue 2003). The cause of this rise in wealth inequality is unclear but it is probably the knock-on effect of the increases in income inequality which took place in the 1980s (Hills 2004). The stock market boom and rise in property prices in the late 1990s are also likely to have had an effect.

So have we become a 'nation of inheritors'? Who is receiving inheritances and from whom, and what is the impact on inequality?

Receipt of inheritance

The most up-to-date and detailed information on receipts of inheritance comes from a nationally-representative survey of 2,008 members of the general public carried out in 2004 (Rowlingson and McKay 2005). The survey found that 46 per cent had received an inheritance at some stage in their lives. If we also include any inheritance received by a partner or any children, then over half the population (53 per cent) lived in families where an inheritance had been received at least once. If we also include lifetime gifts (of at least £500, to exclude 'routine' presents), then approaching two thirds of respondents (63 per cent) had direct or family experience of receiving either an inheritance or such a gift.

Receipts of inheritance therefore seem quite widespread but it is, of course, important to look at the *value* of inheritances. Respondents were asked for the financial value of any inheritance, at the time they received it. Table 2.1 shows both the money and real value of the inheritances people received. Whilst many inheritances were of relatively small value, one person in twenty (five per cent) had inherited something worth at least £50,000 (in today's money) during their lifetime. A further one in ten (nine per cent) had inherited a sum of between £10,000 and £50,000, again in 2004 money. However two per cent had had experiences of inheritance with no financial value at all and 6 per cent with a combined value of under £1,000.

Table 2.1 Receipt of different amounts in an inheritance (by respondents)
Column percentages

	Money values	Real values
No inheritance	54	54
Value not known	9	10
No financial value	2	2
Under £1,000	9	6
£1,000-£4,999	9	8
£5,000-£9,999	4	5
£10,000-£24,999	5	5
£25,000-£49,999	3	4
£50,000-£99,999	2	2
£100,000-£249,999	1	2
£250,000 +	1	1
Unweighted base	2008	2008

Base: All. Some respondents count not give the year of the inheritance, so there are more unknown financial values in the 'real' column.

The amount received through inheritances varied by different social classes as shown in Chart 2.1. Those in middle class occupations were not only more likely to have inherited, but they also had most experience of the larger-valued inheritances. Among social classes A and B (senior and middle-ranking professionals) around one in ten had received an inheritance worth at least £50,000 in today's money. This compares with only one or two per cent among those in classes D and E. This suggests that at present inheritances are not spreading wealth more evenly through the population.

Chart 2.1 Receipt of different real amounts in an inheritance (by social class)

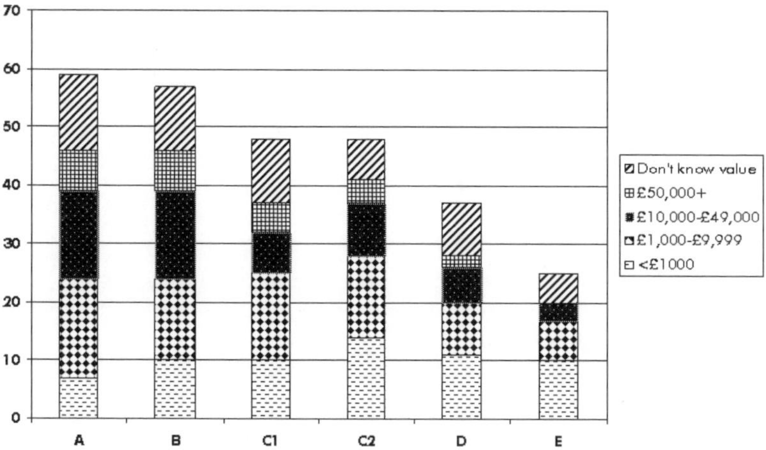

For more detailed analysis we now look separately at each inheritance. This provides greater scope for analysis of the different kinds of items inherited from different people, and the uses to which they were put. In the 2004 survey, about four in ten inheritances were from parents, three in ten from grandparents, one in ten from uncles/aunts, and the remainder from a number of other groups (see Table 2.2). Inheritances of property, however, came overwhelmingly from parents (51 per cent) or from partners (20 per cent). Where personal items had been received, this tended to be as part of an inheritance from grandparents (42 per cent) or from parents (33 per cent).

Table 2.2 Who left the inheritances? Column percentages

	All inheritances received	Property inherited	Money or savings	Personal items
Partner/spouse	6	20	7	5
Parent (or in-law)	39	51	37	33
Grandparent	31	7	28	42
Uncle/aunt	12	12	16	9
Brother/sister	1	1	1	*
Other relative	6	6	6	7
Friend (non-relative)	4	3	5	4
Don't know	1	-	1	-
Unweighted base	1,337	122	499	334

Base: All inheritances received

Transfers of wealth do not just occur at death. If we are interested in the transfer of wealth then we must also consider gifts given throughout life and their impact on inequality. The survey collected data on the giving and receiving of lifetime gifts valued at £500 or more. If these are given prior to the death of the person making the gift, they may be one means of avoiding the bureaucracy and potential tax issues around inheritance. They are also one means by which the donor of the gift may assist their family at a time of their choosing, and perhaps at a time of need of the recipient. The ability to provide sizeable gifts also presupposes that the donor has sufficient confidence in the comfort of their own living standard, and perhaps that future money might be received in the form of an inheritance, too.

Close to one third (31 per cent) of respondents had received gifts worth at least £500. The type of gifts received are shown in Table 2.3 – half this number reported gifts of more than one type.

Table 2.3 Receipt of gifts worth £500 or more

	Percent
Cash to spend	9
Wedding or large social occasion	9
Buying a car	7
Buying (or maintaining) a property	6
Education	5
Paying for driving lessons	4
Birth of children	4
Paying off debts	3
Paying for a holiday (or other luxury)	3
General living expenses	3
Starting a business	1
Other type of gift	2
Cannot remember	1
No, none of these	69
All-any gift worth £500 or more	31
Unweighted base	2008

There was some overlap between receipts of inheritance and receipts of lifetime gifts with 39 per cent of those who had ever inherited also receiving a valuable gift, compared to 23 per cent of those who had not inherited. People are not, therefore, receiving lifetime gifts as some kind of alternative to inheritance, since receipt of the one is positively correlated with receipt of the other. Instead people may be spreading the benefits of the wealth and spending power that is available within their families over time.

Inherited wealth and the inter-generational transmission of inequality

Receipt of inheritance is fairly widespread but the amounts received vary considerably, with those who are already affluent receiving most. This section reviews the impact of inheritance on the transmission of wealth inequality down the generations. Despite some differences of opinion between economists, the main conclusion appears to be that inheritances increase wealth inequality.

Within economics, there has been a long tradition of estimating the effect of bequests on the transmission of wealth inequality. Early studies analysed the values of the estates of fathers and sons. Wedgwood (1939) estimated that one third of the wealthy owed their financial position entirely to the direct effect of inheritance. Harbury and Hitchens (1979) found that 67 per cent of the variance in a son's estate was explained by the variance in a father's estate. But these studies do not prove that inherited wealth is a direct source of inequality because wealthy fathers may pass on other advantages in life which account for their sons' later wealth. Nevertheless, theoretical models by Wilhelm (1997) and empirical work by Menchik (1979) support the conclusion that inheritance is a major source of inequality. Other studies (e.g., Atkinson 1971) have also found that a pure lifecycle model (that is, with no bequests) is unable to explain the upper tail of the wealth distribution, that is, the very wealthy. Hence bequests appear to increase inequality.

Some economists, however, have used simulation models to argue that intergenerational transfers have reduced wealth inequality (see, for example, Stiglitz 1969). But a number of these simulation studies make dubious assumptions. For example, Becker and Tomes (1979) assume that parents leave more money to poorer children than to better-off children. It is therefore no surprise that they find that bequests have an equalising effect both between generations and between siblings. This assumption, however, is not based on any empirical evidence. On the contrary, studies suggest that people bequeath equal amounts to their children in the majority of cases (Finch and Mason 2000). Another common assumption made by economists in this field concerns the absence of assortative mating. Laitner (1979a, b) for example, assumes that rich people are just as likely to partner poor people as other rich people and this, not surprisingly perhaps, accounts for his finding that inheritance is equalising. However, this is another erroneous assumption as it is clear that people live with, and marry, partners of similar socio-economic standing (Ermisch et al 2006).

Some recent studies have utilised more complex simulation models and so have included assumptions such as assortative mating but some dubious assumptions nevertheless remain. For example, Gokhale et al (2001) assume that death is distributed randomly within the population even though it is well known that there are profound socio-economic inequalities in mortality rates (Acheson 1998). However, the study by Gokhale et al (2001) is perhaps the most sophisticated and empirically-grounded simulation model to date. They conclude (2001, pp.124-5) that 'the inheritance of bequests is an important contributor to wealth inequality… We find that skill differences, the annuitisation of retirement savings, assortative mating, and the skewness of the upper tail of the earnings distribution, are the major factors underlying intragenerational wealth inequality.'

It would seem that we are far from becoming a more equal society through inheritance. However, it is undeniable that the growth of owner-occupation has increased the number of people with assets and so it would seem likely that a substantial group of people who might never have expected an inheritance before will now benefit from one. But has the increase in owner-occupation spread the benefits of inheritance more evenly?

Hamnett (1991) carried out a survey in 1988 which demonstrated that 'housing inheritance is strongly class and tenure related … these reflect, rather than reduce, existing patterns of power, privilege and inequality.' He concluded that there had been some redistribution of wealth due to growing owner-occupation but only among the top 50 per cent of the population (that is, from the very wealthiest to the merely affluent). Forrest and Murie (1989) and Forrest and others (1990) similarly accepted that more people might receive something but pointed to the highly differentiated housing market to argue that the value of inheritance would vary greatly. They concluded that even if some working class people received an inheritance it would be a very small one. And the bottom 30 per cent or so of the population are still entirely excluded from this form of wealth and are likely to continue to be excluded, despite recent government attempts to extend home ownership even further.

Given the considerable rise in owner-occupation during the second half of the 20th century we might have expected an upsurge in housing inheritance by the end of that century. Holmans (1997) found that in 1968-9, the Inland Revenue recorded 125,000 estates which included housing assets. This number increased to 149,592 in 1969-70 but then fluctuated year on year with the number of 1992-93 recorded as being 142,446. Hamnett (1997) concludes from this that: 'there has been no increase in the scale of housing inheritance over the last 25 years.' These figures only relate to the number of estates including housing property. They do not tell us how much such estates are worth. Hamnett (1997) estimates that the value of housing in estates increased from £465 million in 1968-69 to a peak of £9.46 billion in 1989-90. House prices fell in the early 1990s but since then there has been a revival in prices and so the value of housing in estates is likely to have increased again. So the value of housing in estates has increased but the number of estates has not. This suggests a concentration of wealth among the 'haves' with the 'have nots' being left further behind.

Why not a 'nation of inheritors'?

The question therefore arises as to why Britain has not become a nation of inheritors.Two main explanations have been put forward.

The first explanation suggests that the cohort of people who became home-owners in the 1980s are not yet old enough to die and pass on their wealth to future generations. Figures from the Office for National Statistics show that those currently aged 80 plus have the lowest rates of owner-occupation of all age groups, except for those under 29. And most people who died in 2000 were 75-84, followed closely by those aged 85 or more.

The second explanation suggests that older people are selling their homes and moving in with their families or into residential care. This would therefore challenge the assumption that there will ever be a move to large numbers of people inheriting. Holmans (1991) estimated that 30,000 older owner-occupier households were dissolved in 1990 through moves to live with relatives or into institutions. He concluded, therefore, that large numbers of people were moving into care and so, under the current English and Welsh system, were having to release housing assets to pay for it. He also suggested, however, that some people might be transferring their house into their children's names prior to death or selling while the owner is in good health to avoid having to pay for care (and/or inheritance tax). Hamnett (1997) concluded that: 'the assumption that most home-owners remain owners until they die is no longer valid.'

Holmans (1997b, p.ix) took account of increasing longevity and use of long-term care when he concluded that although there would be a substantial increase in the number of people receiving inheritances, 'not much more than one half of all non-married men and women even a quarter of a century hence will leave owner-occupied house property'. He felt that this did not justify referring to Britain as a 'nation of inheritors'.

There is, however, one caveat. In more recent years, the use of formal long-term care appears to have decreased. Darton and others (2003) have shown that the late 1990s saw a crisis in long-term care provision as demand for care increased but supply actually declined. For example, the number of care homes fell from just over 17,000 in 1996 to just over 14,000 in 2001. At the same time, fewer people were receiving home-based services. There is a possibility that the trends witnessed by Holmans and Hamnett in the early 1990s have not continued and more people will remain home-owners until they die.

Another reason that inheritances have not spread wealth more evenly through society is the strong support for the concept of family solidarity through inheritance. This is compounded by the fact that wealthier people often partner other people from wealthy backgrounds (assortative mating) and so have double the chance of inheriting (Szydlik, 2004). Furthermore, wealthier people have fewer children and so do not have to split their wealth among so many people. And, finally, wealthier people are more likely to be childless and so might bequeath to nephews and nieces, increasing the chances of some wealthy people inheriting still further. Szydlik analysed the 1996 German Ageing Survey and found that: 'Those who do not have anything generally do not receive anything … the wealthy receive even more wealth, the prosperous become rich, the rich even richer' (2004, p.42).

Wolff (2002) used data from the US Survey of Consumer Finances to analyse inheritances and wealth inequality in the US from 1989-1998. He found that richer households did receive greater inheritances and other wealth transfers than poorer households. But, as a proportion of their current asset-levels, wealth transfers were actually greater for poorer households than richer ones. As he puts it 'a small gift to the poor means more than a large gift to the rich'(2002, p.263). But Wolff does not conclude from this that inheritances reduce wealth inequality because, he argues, poor people tend to spend their small inheritances while rich people are able to add them to their current stock of assets.

Conclusion

Almost half the population have received some form of inheritance but only a small proportion have received substantial inheritances and these people are among the most affluent groups. Those who receive inheritances are also more likely to receive substantial lifetime gifts – further concentrating wealth in the hands of a minority. While the growth of owner-occupation is likely to extend inheritance to a wider group there will still be some, at the bottom, who receive nothing at all and those at the top who receive substantial inheritances. This is due to a range of factors not least the distribution of housing wealth, assortative mating and the tendency for more affluent groups to have fewer, if any, children. This is likely to widen inequalities of wealth still further.

3 | Arguments for Inheritance Tax

Having set out the facts about inheritance, and dispelled some of the myths, we now turn to the arguments for inheritance tax. As we discuss further in Chapter 5, the failure of supporters of the estate tax in the United States to outline a positive *moral* case for the tax was an important factor that contributed to its repeal. We believe there is a strong moral case for inheritance tax in the UK. Drawing out these arguments will be essential in order to construct an effective political case.

We will focus mainly on the following moral arguments for inheritance tax: the tax justice argument; the equality of opportunity argument; and the democratic culture argument. We will also briefly clarify other supporting moral considerations related to the values of political equality, desert, and positive family relations.

The tax justice argument

One argument for inheritance tax appeals to the notion of 'tax justice': of fairness in the distribution of the tax burden. At the outset, we should make clear that we are sceptical of the idea that there is a topic of 'tax justice' that is somehow distinct and/or separable from the broader, background issue of social justice.[1] This cautionary note made, it is important to see how the case for inheritance tax can draw in part from widespread, common-sense notions of tax justice.

One basic thought is this: If someone receives a significant sum, say £300,000, from earnings, and this is subject to taxation, then why should someone who receives the same sum as a wealth transfer, such as an inheritance, not also pay tax? The objection is well stated by Liam Murphy and Thomas Nagel:

'Looked at in this light, the idea that a large gratuitous receipt should not be taxed seems absurd: It would mean that the person who works, gives up leisure, and contributes to economic life must share in society's collective burdens, while the person who gains a windfall without doing anything need not.' (Murphy and Nagel 2001, p.147.)

There are in fact two distinct objections here. One objection is that the failure to tax inheritances (and other wealth transfers) creates what tax economists call a 'horizontal inequity'. It means that there is an arbitrary inequality in the way citizens are treated for tax purposes depending on whether they get transfers from others as earnings or as gifts and inheritances.

The second objection is that the failure to tax inheritances (and other wealth transfers) means that the tax system penalizes relatively virtuous behaviour. Somebody who works and contributes to the social good in this way is doing something virtuous. Somebody who just receives an inheritance or gift is not, as such, doing anything virtuous. But the former person, who is clearly doing something virtuous, pays tax, while the latter person, who is not doing anything virtuous merely in their capacity as a receiver of a gift or inheritance, does not pay tax. How is this fair?

The equality of opportunity argument

The evidence presented in Chapter 2 shows that inheritances are distributed unequally and that this is likely to be a factor in causing inequality of wealth. This suggests that there is likely to be a conflict between the institution of inheritance, in its conventional form, and the value of equality of opportunity.

By equality of opportunity we mean something like this: two children of equal natural ability should have an equal chance to develop and benefit from their skills regardless of the social background of their family (Rawls 1999, p.63). Now wealth confers opportunity in the relevant sense. A person with more wealth has greater opportunity to set up a business, to purchase further and higher education, to undertake unpaid internships so as to get a first step into an area of work, or to travel and make connections and gain inspiration, and so on.[2] Thus, inequality in inheritance translates into inequality of opportunity. Inheritance tax provides a way of neutralizing inequality in wealth inheritances so as to secure greater equality of opportunity.[3]

On the face of it, it looks as if inheritance tax does this in a purely negative or 'levelling down' way, by taking wealth off those who stand to inherit large amounts. The first thing to say here is that it is important to distinguish between levelling down in the space of wealth and in the space of opportunity. If an individual's absolute level of opportunity depends on relative wealth, then mere levelling down of inherited wealth will expand the opportunity of those who would otherwise be at a greater disadvantage in terms of inherited wealth.

For example, imagine three people – Alf, Betty and Carl – who all want a career in journalism. The three have similar abilities, but Betty and Carl use inheritances to finance periods of unpaid internship work which enable them to get valuable work experience and so gain a clear edge over Alf when the three compete for a given job. Imagine now that Betty and Carl do not have these inheritances. The three will now compete on a more level playing-field for the available jobs. Alf might still not get a job, or the job he most wants. But there is a clear sense in which he has more opportunity to get a particular job than in the case where Betty and Carl use their inheritances to get a competitive advantage over him.[4]

Much also depends here on the precise form of the inheritance tax and on what other policies it is combined with. For example, under a lifetime capital receipts tax even a very large estate will pass to others without any tax if the donor transfers the wealth to a large number of people who have not yet received much wealth in this way. For this reason, some argue that it can be expected to have not only a 'levelling down' effect with respect to inherited wealth (preventing the emergence of large inherited fortunes) but a 'levelling up' effect on inherited wealth (promoting a wide dispersion of modest inheritances).

Second, we should distinguish between inheritance as an isolated policy, and inheritance tax as one side of what we may call a *citizens' inheritance scheme* (Paine 1987, Ackerman and Alstott 1999; see also Sandford 1971, Nissan and Le Grand 2000, Paxton and White with Maxwell 2006). We are used to thinking in terms of a familial model of inheritance: we organize the transfer of wealth across the generations via networks of family and friends. But one can also imagine a model of socialized inheritance in which the community takes (some) wealth left on a person's death and uses it to finance the payment of a capital grant to everyone on maturity (or at birth, or at some other point or points in life). Again, under this model there is both a 'levelling down' and a 'levelling up' quality to the overall policy with respect to inherited wealth.

The democratic culture argument

A third important argument focuses on how the failure to tax inheritance (and other wealth transfers) is likely to have a destructive effect on the culture of a democratic society. A democratic society is one in which citizens have a strong sense of themselves as civic and social equals. That is, they see one another as properly commanding equal concern and respect in the eyes of the state and the community. Of course, particular individuals might be esteemed for their achievements in certain areas (e.g., sports, music). But this will go hand in hand with fundamental belief that everyone matters equally. There is no looking down on others as essentially inferior. There is no deference to others merely because of, say, their birth, gender, or ethnicity. A truly democratic society is one in which people can and do look each other in the eye with a shared sense of dignity.

A democratic culture of this kind is arguably desirable, in part, for its own sake (Miller 2000, White 2006). However, it is also important for instrumental reasons. A society which lacks a strong democratic culture might well be less able to sustain just social institutions. If people lack a strong sense of the fundamental equality of their fellow citizens, they are likely to be less inclined to support the policies which express this equality. Related to this, a society which lacks a strong democratic culture might be more conflictual. Social interactions might well become more infused with feelings of mutual resentment. In the extreme, such feelings could jeopardize social and political stability.

The failure to tax inheritances (and other wealth transfers) might well contribute to a steady corrosion of democratic culture. Quite simply, those who inherit large sums thereby experience society in a fundamentally different way to those who do not. They get things – or, at least, some important things – more easily than others. Combined with a sense of entitlement this can easily lead to a sense of belonging to a distinct and superior social class. The basic point is expressed eloquently by R.H. Tawney in his *Equality*:

> One of the regrettable...effects of extreme inequality is its tendency to weaken the capacity for impartial judgement. It pads the lives of its beneficiaries with a soft down of consideration...and secures that, if they fall, they fall on cushions. It disposes them, on the one hand, to take for granted themselves and their own advantages, as though there were nothing in the latter which could possibly need explanation, and, on the

other hand, to be critical of claims to similar advantages advanced by their neighbours who do not yet possess them. It causes them, in short, to apply different standards to different sections of the community, as if it were uncertain whether all of them are human in the same sense as themselves. (Tawney 1964, pp.37-38.)

Other considerations

In addition to the above three arguments, we may note a number of further moral considerations which support inheritance tax.

First, we should bear in mind the connection between wealth distribution and political equality. Political equality refers to the equality of citizens to participate in political decision-making. There is a long tradition of republican political thought which sees wealth inequality as a potential threat to this basic democratic norm (Thompson 2007). In various ways, the rich can and do buy voice and influence and this can undermine the substantive equality in participation rights which is essential to democratic politics. As John Rawls puts it: '...when inequalities of wealth exceed a certain limit...political liberty...tends to lose its value, and representative government to become such in appearance only' (Rawls 1999, p.246). While there might be a number of ways of addressing this problem, inheritance tax can conceivably have a role to play in limiting the gradual accumulation of very large fortunes over time and can thereby help reduce the pressure on political equality from this source (Rawls 1999, pp.245-246).

Second, and somewhat anticipated in our discussion of the tax justice argument, is the idea of desert. It is widely believed that a just distribution of income and wealth should bear some reasonable approximation to personal desert (Miller 2000). The failure to tax inheritance, however, will tend to push the distribution of wealth away from a reasonable approximation to desert. People who get little or no inheritance might, for this reason, have to work hard in demanding jobs to get a decent standard of living. Meanwhile, receipt of a large inheritance can release someone from the need to work at all. It can be the platform for a life of self-indulgence. This consideration helps explain why it is not only left-wing egalitarians who favour inheritance tax (for the sort of reasons outlined above), but also some reflective thinkers on the right.

Third, and to anticipate a point to which we will return in the next chapter, the inheritance system also has implications for the quality of family relations. Consider the way in which someone can use the threat of disinheritance to cajole others into behaviour of which they approve.

Or consider the way in which the prospect of an inheritance can generate ugly rivalry between family members jostling for favour. Inheritance tax reduces what is at stake in such cases and so also reduces the incentive to engage in such behaviour. Thus, while a concern for 'family values' probably tells against extremely high levels of inheritance tax (as we will discuss in the next chapter), some level of inheritance tax might actually be good for family relations.

4 | Objections to inheritance tax

In the previous chapter we saw that there is a strong case for inheritance tax. However, it is the objections to the tax that loom larger in the public debate. This chapter considers three important objections to the tax. Building an effective case for inheritance tax will mean testing these objections and identifying counter arguments. As we noted in Chapter 1, opposition to inheritance tax is primarily grounded in moral concerns, concerns which played a major role in the debate leading to the repeal of the estate tax in the United States. So this chapter also examines the two main moral objections to inheritance tax: that it is unfair because it results in 'double taxation'; and that it is unfair because it penalizes virtuous behaviour. There is also a pragmatic objection which focuses on the possible impact of the tax on incentives to work and save.

The double tax objection: It is unfair for someone who has already paid tax on an income to then have to pay a second tax on assets which have been saved out of the already-taxed income.

The public opinion work reviewed in Chapter 1 suggests that one of the most important – in the sense of widely-held – moral objections to inheritance tax is that it is unfair because it is a 'double tax'. What can be said in reply to this objection? Here we note some of the possible replies.

First, the double tax objection seems to suppose that inheritance tax falls *on the same person* who has previously paid tax on income from which he or she has made some savings which he or she is now passing on to another as an inheritance. But in the case of a capital receipts tax (or an inheritance tax in the strict sense of the term), this assumption obviously doesn't hold (Patrick and Jacobs 2003, p.9). The tax is paid by the recipient, not by the donor. So how can the tax be a second tax of or on the donor?

To come at the point another way, consider the following parallel case. Say I earn £x a year on which I pay some tax. I now employ Jones as a plumber to fix a pipe in my kitchen. I pay her £y for this, and she pays a tax on this £y. Does the fact that the plumber pays tax on a transfer she got from me, a transfer out of income which had already been taxed, make *this* a case of double taxation? It seems absurd to say so. But structurally the case seems no different to the case in which the £y is, say, a capital receipt out of somebody else's estate (which has been saved out of taxed earnings).

A follow up point to the first reply is this: in fact, whether the inheritance tax takes the form of a capital receipts tax or an estate tax, it is always in effect the recipient who pays it (Patrick and Jacobs 2003, p.9, McLean 2007). This is obvious in the case of the capital receipts tax, but what about the estate tax? Quite simply, the 'donor' under an estate tax cannot pay the tax because he or she is dead. Dead people don't do very much, and that includes paying taxes. Even under an estate tax, the tax itself is still in effect paid by the recipients of the estate.

It might be argued that the foregoing analysis is too static: that it ignores the way people might change their behaviour in anticipation of a tax that will be paid by recipients of a wealth transfer. If I know that my children will pay tax on a wealth transfer then I might increase the amount I transfer to them to offset this, curtailing my own consumption (or saving for other purposes) by this offsetting amount. Am I not then, in effect, carrying the burden of the tax even if I am not, strictly speaking, the one who pays it? In which case, couldn't there be a germ of truth in the double tax objection? Note, however, that this version of the double tax objection gets off the ground only if one makes specific behavioural assumptions. Note also that the assumption one must apparently make to float this version of the double tax objection (people save more to offset tax) is the opposite of the assumption one must make to float the usual incentives objection to inheritance tax (people save less because their bequests will be taxed). This implies that there is a tension involved in trying to press both objections simultaneously.

Even if we could put the foregoing points aside, a further problem arises. This is that those who press the double tax objection against inheritance tax typically press it against this particular tax without considering whether the logic of the objection implicates other taxes and without explaining why the objection is less important in relation to these other taxes. As it is usually presented, and even if we accept the (highly questionable) characterisation of inheritance tax as a double tax, the objection is *arbitrarily selective* in its focus on inheritance tax in particular.

One possible response is to argue that all other taxes which apparently involve double taxation (e.g. sales taxes) are equally objectionable as inheritance tax (Prabhakar 2008a). This response might itself take either a weak or a strong form.

In its strong form, the response holds that the government may never adopt a tax if it involves double taxation (*because* it involves double taxation). But in view of the range of taxes it would rule out (e.g. sales taxes) this is clearly an absurd conclusion.

In its weak form, the response holds that all taxes which involve double taxation are, for this reason, equally undesirable, but that some of them might nevertheless be adopted if the overall balance of reasons favours this. In other words, it *counts against* adopting a given tax that it involves double taxation, but it doesn't necessarily count *decisively* against it if the tax serves some other, sufficiently important public interest. If this is so, however, then the double tax objection would, of course, no longer necessarily count decisively against inheritance tax. It would be open to the supporter of inheritance tax to argue that the reasons favouring the tax – such as equality of opportunity – are strong enough to justify the tax even though it is a double tax and, in this specific respect, undesirable.

There is, however, another possible response to the point that taxes other than inheritance tax involve double taxation. Since double taxation is apparently ubiquitous, implicating all kinds of taxes, this might prompt one to reconsider whether it really is objectionable as such after all. Once we do this, it is by no means clear that it is objectionable as such. The point is put very well by Liam Murphy and Thomas Nagel:

> Taxes are not like punishments, which may not be imposed twice for the same crime....Multiple distinct taxes often tax people's assets "twice," as when a sales tax is imposed on the expenditure of someone's after-tax income, or a property tax is collected on an asset that was bought with income subject to tax. Any issues of fairness in such cases would have to be about the cumulative effect of multiple taxes, not about double taxation *per se*. (Murphy and Nagel 2001, p.143.)

To conclude: in reply to the double tax objection we can say: (1) that inheritance tax does not necessarily involve double taxation; and (2) that even if it does, it is not clear that double taxation as such is unfair.

The virtue objection: inheritance tax is unfair because it penalizes virtuous behaviour relative to selfish/'vicious' behaviour.

Another worry that informs opposition to inheritance is the thought that the tax penalizes behaviour that seems virtuous and praiseworthy. To see this, consider a simple example (based on McCaffery 1994, p.296). Imagine two people, Spender and Bequeather, each of whom has a fortune of £10 million. Each knows that he or she has about a year to live. Spender chooses to consume all of his wealth before his death. Bequeather chooses to save all of her fortune to pass on to her children at her death. Intuitively, many people would regard Spender's behaviour as rather *selfish* (at least if he too, as we may assume, has children), whereas Bequeather's behaviour appears loving and, therefore, as much more *virtuous*. Yet, so the argument goes, inheritance tax hits Bequeather, who apparently acts virtuously in saving her wealth for her children, while Spender remains free selfishly to consume his wealth without any tax. Hence we get the idea that inheritance tax is distinctively objectionable because it is a 'tax on virtue' or a 'tax on love' (McCaffery 1994).

What can be said in reply to this objection? To begin with, we should recall the point we made in Chapter 3: given that labour income is taxed, the failure to tax inheritances and other wealth transfers also apparently penalizes relatively virtuous behaviour. In this situation, if Smith works to earn £x she will pay tax on this, while if Jones receives a gift or inheritance of £x, she pays no tax. Yet Smith is doing something virtuous in working for her £x while Jones, merely in her capacity as a recipient of a gift or inheritance, does nothing virtuous. Hence, even if we accept that the virtue objection as just presented is a forceful objection to inheritance tax, it would not necessarily be a decisive objection because there is also a strong virtue-based objection to *not* having an inheritance tax.

But is the virtue objection, as just presented, as forceful as it appears? There are a number of reasons to question this.

First, what we need to focus on is the impact of the tax system as a whole, not just at the impact of one specific tax. For the unequal burden implied by one tax might be balanced by the unequal impact of some other tax, so that the tax system as a whole might not burden virtuous behaviour relative to selfish behaviour even if inheritance tax by itself does. In this case, for example, the tax that Bequeather pays (putting to one side the point that the dead cannot actually pay taxes) might be balanced by sales or consumption taxes paid by Spender.

Second, the virtue objection presents saving/bequest behaviour as clearly virtuous and consumption behaviour as clearly selfish. But this is far too simplistic. Returning once more to Spender and Bequeather, imagine the story goes like this. Spender lives modestly for most of the year except for one memorable weekend when he throws a huge farewell party for his family and friends. Over many years, Bequeather has subtly, but effectively, threatened to cut her children out of her will if they choose careers different to the ones she thinks suitable. Her subtle threats have had their desired effect: in middle age, they are embedded in careers that they would not have chosen were it not for the threat of disinheritance, though they have adapted their preferences to their lot. (Of course, their situation is even worse if inheritance law allows Bequeather to set conditions on the receipt of her estate, allowing the threat of disinheritance a zombie-like afterlife when she is dead.) Now, where do we think the balance of 'selfishness' and 'virtue' lies? Bequeather's manipulative use of her estate to control others – surely a far from implausible scenario when it comes to the family politics of inheritance – seems far more 'selfish' and lacking in virtue than Spender's life-affirming choice to throw his family and friends a great farewell party.

Moreover, as we have already noted, the institution of private inheritance can in various other ways encourage selfish or otherwise 'vicious' motivation and behaviour. It can lead to ugly competition between family members to secure favoured standing in the eyes of the parent or grandparent with a large estate. It can underpin, and so encourage, lives of vacuous underachievement by those who inherit large fortunes, one reason why some commentators on the right have historically criticized the institution (Rowlingson 2008). As we noted in Chapter 3, insofar as inheritance tax diminishes what is at stake in such cases, it can be expected to dampen down, to help discourage, these particular 'vicious' feelings and behaviours.

So far we have challenged the assumed link between saving/bequest behaviour and virtue by appealing to rather uncontroversial ideas about what is virtuous, selfish, and so on. However, the reply to the virtue objection is strengthened if we bring into the discussion values like equality of opportunity and consider what they imply for our understanding of virtue and vice.

To get at the point, let's pose a question: Putting issues of manipulation etc. to one side, does a parent necessarily act virtuously in wishing to leave as much wealth as possible to his/her children?

In answering the question we have to balance two plausible intuitions. The first intuition is that the parent-child relationship is properly constrained by demands of justice, including the demand for equal opportunity, and that this sets some limits on how parents can act to provide advantage for their children. Widely shared norms against 'nepotism' in employment reflect this idea. The second intuition is that it is morally incredible to suppose that parents should not be allowed to do *anything* which results in their children having relative advantage over other children, or even to suppose that they *always* do something morally wrong when their actions have this effect. To cite the example used by Harry Brighouse and Adam Swift in their ongoing exploration of this issue, we should not prevent parents from reading bedtime stories to their children, or even criticize them on moral grounds for doing so, even if the effect of this is to give their children advantage relative to other children (Brighouse and Swift, forthcoming).

In the case of inheritance tax, we can understand the idea that in order to express and enjoy the kind of special intimacy that characterizes family relationships, family members do need to be able to pass certain items of emotional significance down the generations. Family members surely ought to have some freedom to pass on such items, without the shadow of tax liability, even if the effect is to cause some inequality in wealth inheritances. The critical question, however, is *how much* we should be allowed to pass on and/or receive. If the concern for family intimacy supports a movement away from a notional policy of 100 per cent taxation of wealth transfers, this does not mean a policy of 0 per cent taxation is therefore appropriate. We would argue that the intimacy interest in wealth transfers identified here does support a policy of exempting some level of bequest or capital receipt from tax, but that the exemption should also be limited in order to accommodate (albeit partially) the claims of equal opportunity.

If parents complain that such limits penalize the 'virtuous' desire to benefit their children, then we can reply that beyond these limits the desire is not virtuous at all. It is a desire lacking in virtue precisely because it intends, or can reasonably be expected, to put their children at a serious relative advantage compared to others' children, thereby placing undue strain on society's achievement of equality of opportunity.

The incentives objection: inheritance tax is undesirable because it creates disincentives to work and save.

Even if one thinks that inheritance tax is fair in principle, one might oppose it in practice because one fears that it will create disincentives to work and save. This thought lies behind the incentives objection.

Before replying to the objection, two points need to be made. First, since many taxes have disincentive effects of some kind, anyone pressing such an objection against inheritance tax in particular must argue not only that this tax has disincentive effects, but that it has greater disincentive effects than other taxes which we might cut. Merely pointing to its supposed disincentive effects does not give us a reason to cut inheritance tax, or abolish it, rather than, say, cutting income tax by an equivalent amount.

Second, anyone pressing the objection needs to make clear just how and why the alleged disincentive effects matter. An obvious answer is: 'Because in the long-run they result in lower output in the aggregate.' But lower output overall need not imply lower income or opportunity for everyone. Even if an egalitarian tax regime lowers aggregate output in the long-term, it might at the same time raise the long-term income and/or opportunity of the least advantaged in society. The income/opportunity of this specific group might be higher than it would be under a less egalitarian tax regime which produces higher output in the aggregate. So at what point, exactly, do disincentives matter? When they reduce aggregate output? Or when they specifically reduce the prospects of, say, the least advantaged in society?

Proponents of the objection need to clarify which of a wide range of possible criteria they are using to identify when disincentive effects count decisively against a tax. For the different possible criteria are likely to have very different policy implications. Here we note that a criterion of simple output maximization is hardly credible: it is not plausible to think that all that matters is how much output an economy generates over the long-term regardless of how this output is distributed.

Let us now turn to the underlying claim that inheritance tax does have disincentive effects on work and/or saving. What are we to make of this claim?

First, we should note that economic theory provides no clear prediction about the likely effect of inheritance tax and similar taxes (Tait 1967, pp.167-194, Holtz-Eakin 1996, Wolff 1996, Gale and Perozek 2001). On the one hand, the tax does increase the effective relative price of saving one's wealth for bequest or transfer purposes as against consuming the wealth. But as every economist knows, this 'substitution effect' has to be set against a possible 'income effect': in this context, this refers to the fact that if an individual wishes to pass a certain amount of wealth on to others, the tax will make it necessary to save even more in order to do so. There is no way of saying in purely theoretical terms which of these effects will be the largest, and so whether the tax will result in more or less work and saving.

In addition, one needs to keep in mind the possible disincentive effects of *allowing* inheritances free of tax. The knowledge that one is going to get a large inheritance can obviously act as a disincentive to work and save oneself. Why make an effort to work or save knowing that one can rely on the fruits of parental or grandparental saving? So even if the net effect of an inheritance tax is to reduce work and saving amongst those in one generation who wish to leave wealth to their family, this might be offset to some extent – conceivably, more than offset – by the damage to the work/saving incentives of younger people who stand to get the inheritances.

The only way we can sort out the overall effect of inheritance tax on work and savings, given the indeterminacy of the issue in purely theoretical terms, is to look at the available empirical research. Does this research support the incentives objection?

In fact, the research evidence in this area is rather thin. Economists have researched the motivation behind bequests in some depth. Perhaps unsurprisingly, the main finding seems to be that no single, simple theory of why people leave bequests is adequate. Nor does existing research point to significant large, negative effects on work or saving from existing inheritance taxes (Holtz-Eakin 1996). To be clear, we cannot say that inheritance tax has no such effects. We simply don't know much about how far it has such effects.

Thus, while it seems common sense to say that *some level* of inheritance tax will have undesirable disincentive effects on work and/or saving, we have little theoretical or empirical sense of exactly what this level is. We certainly have little reason, purely on incentives grounds, to think that the best level of inheritance tax is 0 per cent.

Conclusion

We have reviewed three important objections to inheritance tax. None of them offers a decisive objection to the tax. So far as we can see, the double tax objection has very little, if any, merit, despite its wide currency. The incentives and virtue objections point to considerations which count against extremely high levels of inheritance tax (e.g. 100 per cent taxation), but they do not seriously call into question the principle of inheritance tax.

“

5 | Moving Forward

We have set out a compelling case for inheritance tax. However, inheritance tax is unpopular. So what prospect is there for progress? Although regrettable in itself, the government's decision in October 2007 to raise the thresholds for inheritance tax might at least have the advantage of buying some time to popularise the arguments for the tax and to consider more desirable reforms to the tax. How can we seize this opportunity?

We begin this chapter by noting some important qualifications concerning existing studies of public opinion on the issue. We then consider what lessons can be learned from the recent struggle over the estate tax in the United States. Drawing on these insights we then set out some basic principles of political strategy for the defence of inheritance tax. Finally, we set out a strategy based on these principles.

We argue for a strategy based on:

1. A switch to a lifetime capital receipts tax;
2. Linkage of a reformed inheritance tax to the 'equal life chances' agenda already advanced by the government in other contexts;
3. Strengthening of this link by connecting the tax in public discussion to specific spending commitments, e.g., to pre-school intervention programs;
4. The development of a citizen-led, public campaign for tax fairness, bringing together trade unions, anti-poverty groups, and others to contest the claims of anti-tax groups such as the Taxpayers' Alliance.

Public opinion revisited

In Chapter 1 we noted that inheritance tax is unpopular. However, the finding of unpopularity must be set in the context of the general public's sketchy knowledge of the tax. Karen Rowlingson and Stephen McKay (2005) conducted a survey of 2008 people on attitudes to inheritance for the Joseph Rowntree Foundation. This study discovered that people have very poor knowledge of inheritance tax. For example, they found that only 19 per cent of their respondents had anything like a reasonably accurate idea of the tax that would have to be paid if a widow leaves an estate of £300,000 for her children. This lack of knowledge casts doubt on the idea that there is an *informed* public debate about inheritance tax. This can fuel misconceptions about who actually is liable and actually pays this tax. Rowlingson and McKay suggest that an obvious step to improve the public debate is to provide greater information about this tax. This would then allow people to engage properly with arguments about inheritance tax.

Second, existing studies tend to ask the public about their attitudes to inheritance tax in isolation from other taxes. No tax is likely to court immediate popularity as they represent a cost upon individuals. This resistance is compounded by the finding from the Fabian Society's Commission on Taxation and Citizenship (2000) which reveals that people feel that their taxes are not being spent well by government. This means that the opposition to inheritance tax is unsurprising given that it is part of a broader concern with all taxes.

However, this raises the question of whether inheritance tax is more unpopular than other taxes. Answering this question requires asking people to weigh-up the merits of inheritance tax against other taxes. Rajiv Prabhakar (2008a, 2008b) provides some evidence which suggests public attitudes are more complex once this is done. He conducted 7 focus groups with 58 members of the public in England in 2006 to investigate attitudes to wealth taxes. As part of this participants were asked to choose one of two packages: a tax system in which cuts in income tax would be off-set by rises in inheritance tax, or a system in which rises in income tax would finance a cut in inheritance tax. The aim here was to see if attitudes to inheritance tax shifted once this tax was placed in a broader context of other taxes. Prabhakar found that opinion was split over these options. Some favoured having a higher income tax with their descendants paying a lower duty on the final estate. However, this is offset by a significant strand of opinion that backs cutting income tax and raising inheritance tax.

Third, existing studies offer some support for the thesis that support for inheritance tax is increased when the tax is linked to specific spending commitments (Lewis and White 2006).

Lessons from the United States

In 2001, George Bush repealed estate tax in the United States. This was a shock to many in the US as inherited privilege had never been popular in a country where individuals were supposed to secure the American Dream through their own efforts. The tax had existed for over a century and only 2 per cent of the richest Americans paid it. But the repeal lobby managed to build an unlikely and broad alliance against the 'Death Tax' (as they called it). The key to their campaign was a moral case against the tax, illustrated with a few well-chosen narratives. The opposition fought back, ineffectively, with pragmatic arguments and statistics.

From the late 19th century onwards, the moral high-ground in the US had been occupied by those in favour of estate tax. People were expected to make their own fortunes rather than rely on inheriting the fortunes of their parents. Bequests were thought to make young people idle and profligate. And rich people were expected to give their money to good causes rather than hoard it for their own children. In addition, society was seen to have a claim on inherited wealth because it had provided the economic conditions, rules of law and security to allow wealth to grow. However, during the 1990s, those wishing to repeal estate tax began to gain a foothold on the moral high-ground by arguing that the wealth accumulated during a lifetime was the sovereign possession of the owner to dispose of as they like. One of the tactics for changing opinions on this particular issue was to re-label estate tax as the 'death tax' and to take an absolute stand against the principle of double taxation.

The repealers did not rely solely on an abstract moral case. They also drew on narrative case studies such as that involving Chester Thigpen, an African American 'grandchild of slaves' who had worked hard to build up a farm. Chester was in his 80s and was worried about whether or not his farm would be able to pass intact to his children when he died. Stories such as this were powerful because they stimulated empathy. They involved relatively average Americans, not multi-millionaires. They involved people who had worked hard and had strong family values. These stories were not necessarily representative or common but they struck a chord with a wide range of middle America as well as those with great wealth.

The moral argument and narrative accounts attracted a large and diverse lobby. Public opinion surveys were used by repealers to demonstrate widespread support for their cause. Surveys also found that the estate tax was especially unpopular among disadvantaged minorities, because it could be portrayed as penalising those, like Chester Thigpen, who had overcome many obstacles to accumulate their wealth. Similar arguments were used to win the support of gay men and lesbians who would also have to overcome barriers to accumulate wealth and who were then doubly discriminated against due to their inability to take advantage of marital tax deductions. The lobby was also powerful with many very rich Americans financing the campaign (though doing so fairly quietly to avoid the accusation of self-interest).

So the repealers had moral arguments, narrative accounts and strong support from a large, diverse and powerful lobby. What about the opposition? Rather than construct a positive moral case for inheritance tax the anti-repealers tended to call on self-interest. For example, they argued that only 2 per cent of Americans had to pay it so it would not affect many people. They produced reams of statistics to back up their case. But the appeal to self-interest, backed up by statistics, failed to resonate when up against the fairness arguments of the tax's opponents, supported by compelling individual narratives.

Thus far, the debate in the UK has shown signs of following a similar path. Much recent campaigning against inheritance tax has drawn on claims about fairness. For example, an online petition[1] submitted by a *Daily Express* journalist began by claiming that inheritance tax was 'immoral' on the basis that it may penalise hard work. The *Daily Express* has not been alone in putting forward moral arguments against inheritance tax. In August 2006, a former New Labour cabinet minister, Stephen Byers, echoed the newspaper when he called inheritance tax 'a penalty on hard work, thrift and enterprise'.[2] The main group campaigning against inheritance tax is the Taxpayers' Alliance, whose Director, James Frayne, has said on their web-site:

'Inheritance tax is unfair and it is starting to hit more and more ordinary families across the country, rather than the rich who have the funds to come up with ways of avoiding it. Unless the leadership of all the main parties commit themselves to abolishing it as part of a programme to ease the tax burden they are going to find themselves increasingly out of touch with voters.'[3]

The UK campaign against inheritance tax has also attempted to employ some narrative case studies. For example, two elderly sisters (Joyce and Sybil Burden) have fought for the same inheritance tax rights as married and civil partnered couples.[4] The sisters have lived together since birth but are concerned that when one of them dies the other will have to pay inheritance tax on her sister's share of the estate. They fear that this might necessitate sale of the family home to pay the tax bill. The sisters decided to take action after the Civil Partnership Act 2004 came into operation. It granted the same rights to civil partnered gay and lesbian couples as married couples have. The Burden sisters believed that this amounted to discrimination under the terms of the European Convention of Human Rights. Their case went all the way to the European Court which ruled against the women in December 2006 by a majority of four to three but with strong dissenting judgments. The sisters are currently appealing to the Grand Chamber.

Until recently, the main supporters of inheritance tax have been the Treasury. It responded to the attack by Stephen Byers by saying: 'Inheritance tax is a fair and necessary means of raising revenue for public services, and only affects the top 6 per cent of all estates.'[5] Other Labour government members at the time, such as Alistair Darling (who was then Trade and Industry Secretary) also defended inheritance tax by saying that Byers' stance 'may make for a headline, but it doesn't make for a prudent and sensible tax-and-spend policy.' Although the Treasury response makes reference to fairness, no effort is made to explain why the tax is fair. The emphasis in such responses is on self-interest ('Don't worry, few people pay this tax') and pragmatism ('We need the money this tax raises'). This emphasis did not work in the US and it became clear in October 2007 that it is not going to work in the UK either.

So what is the alternative?

Political strategy

What lessons can we draw from looking again at public opinion and the dynamics of estate tax repeal in the US? The following seem to be the main lessons:

1. Public opinion is generally not well-informed about the nature and incidence of the tax. So a political strategy for the defence of inheritance tax must seek to increase basic information about the tax, its incidence, and its effects.
2. The experience of the US suggests, however, that it is not adequate to

defend inheritance tax merely by citing statistics and appealing to self-interest. Opposition to the tax derives its force from the perceived unfairness of the tax. So supporters of the tax must set out the moral arguments for the tax and explain the flaws in the moral arguments of the critics.

3. Moral argument itself can be rather abstract. It needs to be strengthened by means of supporting 'narratives' which make the abstract points of principle concrete and accessible.
4. Discussion of inheritance tax must be related to the tax system as a whole.
5. Discussion of inheritance tax should be related to spending commitments. Linking inheritance tax in political argument to specific spending commitments can provide the basis for accessible narratives that help to clarify, and build support for, the ends of inheritance tax.
6. Inheritance tax itself should be designed in ways that help to defuse potential moral objections to the tax.
7. Opposition to inheritance tax has been reinforced by citizen-led groups lobbying government and intervening in the media to shape the climate of public debate. A citizen-led, public campaigning approach is essential to defend the tax and a fair tax system in general.

Moving forward: a lifetime capital receipts tax

The first requirement of a strategy to defend inheritance tax is to get the tax itself right. The present inheritance tax, which is really an estate tax, has reached the end of the road. The time has come to replace it with a capital receipts tax. This has long been an objective of progressive tax reformers.

One model of such a tax is a lifetime capital receipts tax. This allows each person a reasonable lifetime quota of wealth which he or she can receive without tax. Wealth transfers above the quota are then subject to tax, perhaps at a progressive rate. The Fabian Society's Commission on Taxation and Citizenship, which reported in 2000, provides an example of what such a tax might look like in practice (Fabian Society, 2000, see also Patrick and Jacobs, 2003). This is modelled in part on the Capital Acquisition Tax in Ireland, introduced in 1976.[6] The main features of the Commission on Taxation and Citizenship's scheme are as follows:

- Recipients are allowed to receive up to £80,000 over their lifetime in gifts and inheritances without any tax liability.
- A progressive tax is imposed on anything above £80,000.
- Amounts between £80,000 to £160,000 are taxed at 20 per cent.
- Sums between £160,000 to £240,000 are taxed at 30 per cent.
- Anything above £240,000 is taxed at 40 per cent.

In any given year, individuals are able to receive £2,000 gifts tax-free. Multiple donations from one person to another would count as one gift. This is to prevent a donor who wishes to give more than £2,000 from trying to avoid this tax by dividing their gift into separate £2,000 slices.

The precise thresholds and rates are of course a matter for further discussion, but the Fabian proposal at least gives us a concrete illustration of how the lifetime capital receipts tax would work. A lifetime capital receipts tax seems preferable to an estate tax for a number of reasons.

First, it addresses more directly our fairness concerns about inheritance. Unequal receipt of inheritances over the life course is a cause of unequal opportunity and hence a potential block to social mobility. By targeting receipts, rather than estates, a capital receipts tax focuses on what we are really concerned about. This makes the moral point of taxing wealth transfers much clearer.

Second, it removes one major source of tax avoidance. Under the present estate tax, no tax is paid on wealth which is given away more than seven years before death. This provides another important means of avoiding the tax which reduces its effectiveness and detracts from its legitimacy. But under a lifetime capital receipts tax these transfers would still count as part of an individual's record of receipts and so would be subject to tax (once the individual's tax-free quota is exceeded).

Third, a capital receipts tax seems obviously less vulnerable to the double tax objection to inheritance tax. The tax is explicitly paid by the recipient of the inheritance and so it makes little sense to portray it as a 'second tax' on the person who has died (unless, perhaps, this person adjusted his or her own saving to negate the effect of the tax).

Fourth, because the tax paid on an estate under a capital receipts tax depends on how widely it is distributed, many have argued that a capital receipts tax gives people an incentive to spread their wealth more widely. It not only levels down very large inheritances but encourages a wider distribution of inheritances. Some critics have doubted how powerful this incentive is likely to be (Elster 1986). But even if it is quite small it still represents a gain in terms of the proper fairness goals of the tax system.

There are two main objections against a shift to a lifetime capital receipts tax. The first is that a capital receipts tax will raise less tax revenue than an estate tax. Imagine someone gives away a fortune of £1m. Under an estate tax, the amount of tax paid depends simply on the size of the estate and is unaffected by how the donor chooses to divide up the estate. But under the capital receipts tax, the donor can split the estate up so as to minimize the tax liability, e.g., by dividing the sum into a lot of small inheritances.

There are a number of replies to this. First, the revenue effects of a switch from an estate to a capital receipts tax will obviously depend in part on what thresholds and tax rates we choose for the new tax. The objection must be that a switch to a capital receipts tax at any *politically feasible* set of thresholds and rates will cause a net fall in tax revenue relative to an estate tax with a similar level of political feasibility. However, it is by no means obvious that this will occur. For the effect we noted above will be offset to some extent – possibly more than offset – by the fact that a lifetime capital receipts tax has a wider tax base: the tax applies to gifts made well before death, which is not the case under the present estate tax (Atkinson 1972).

Further, even if the switch to a capital receipts tax does lead to a net fall in tax revenue, this is not a decisive objection. To some extent, this might reflect a tendency to distribute estates more widely in response to the incentives created by the tax, and this should be welcomed. Moreover, even if the immediate effect is to reduce revenue, relative to the present estate tax, this is an acceptable price to pay for getting a tax on wealth transfers which has the advantages described above, advantages which make the tax more politically defensible than an estate tax in the long-run.

The second main objection to a lifetime capital receipts tax is that it is administratively complex and expensive.

There is no doubt that a lifetime capital receipts tax *is* more administratively complex (and hence, likely to be more expensive to collect) than the current estate tax. The tax authorities no longer have to track estates but inheritances and bequests, which will outnumber estates.

They no longer have to look just at wealth transferred at death, but at gifts. To assess tax liability, they must consider not only the size of the gift or inheritance, but how much someone has already received by way of gift or inheritance. In each of these ways, a lifetime capital receipts tax is more informationally demanding, and so more complex and costly to administer, than an estate tax.

This is, however, by no means a decisive objection to a lifetime capital receipts tax. Previous studies of the issue have indicated that the tax is both administratively feasible and that its administrative cost, while certainly higher than that of an estate tax, is unlikely to be out of line with the average administrative cost of taxes in the UK (Atkinson, 1972, Sandford, Willis and Ironside, 1973). As noted, the Irish Republic has had a similar tax since 1976 and the fact that it has been in operation for over thirty years now suggests that it is not administratively unfeasible or prohibitively costly.[7]

Moving forward: the wider strategy

Getting the tax itself right is the first, crucial step in defending inheritance tax. But it is only the first step. To move forward effectively, we must link the reformed tax clearly to a wider public philosophy of equality of life chances; we should make this link even more explicit by connecting the tax in public discussion with initiatives that clearly help to widen life chances; and we must build a citizen-led campaign to support tax fairness, rather than expecting government alone to make the case for the tax.

Our discussion suggests (see Chapter 3) that the idea of equality of opportunity logically has to lie at the core of the moral case for inheritance tax. One key issue, therefore, concerns how the commitment to equal opportunity can be communicated in a clear and compelling way. One suggestion, from the Fabian Society's Commission on Life Chances and Child Poverty (2006), is to try to build a story based on *equal life chances for all*. This focuses on the barriers and challenges faced by many families, particularly those on low incomes, to give their children the best start in life, and to provide the kind of stimulating and enjoyable experiences and opportunities which more advantaged families take for granted. The aim is to get debates away from the very rich or very poor and focus instead onto tackling inequality and providing equal life chances for the bulk of families who face daily obstacles to providing comparable opportunities for their children to the more affluent. There is some recent evidence to suggest that this life chances approach may be useful for forming a coalition of support for policies that spread opportunity (Castell and Thompson 2007). Such a story is readily connected with existing government initiatives to end child poverty and to reduce class inequalities in higher educational achievement.

One way to reinforce the connection between a reformed inheritance tax and the equal life chances agenda is to link the tax in public discussion with spending programs that have the equalization of life chances as a clear objective.

One possibility which has been suggested is to link a reformed inheritance tax to spending on a universal grant scheme like the government's Child Trust Fund (Commission on Taxation and Citizenship 2000, Nissan and Le Grand 2000, Patrick and Jacobs 2003). Under the Child Trust Fund all children receive a small sum at birth (£250 for most children, £500 for poorer children) which is held in trust to accumulate for them as they grow up. The state makes additional payments into the accounts at age seven, and families may add up to £1,200 per year (HM Treasury 2003). Some argue that linking inheritance tax to such a scheme will show how the tax is ultimately about spreading opportunity not simply diminishing it for some people. However, there is evidence that this particular linkage might not be that effective in building support for a reformed inheritance tax (Lewis and White 2006). The Child Trust Fund represents a new departure in social policy, and some people worry about how young people might use their funds at age 18. Moral intuitions about equal opportunity and responsible behaviour come apart.

An obvious alternative is to link the tax in public discussion with preschool intervention programs which aim to address physical, emotional and cognitive disadvantage at an early stage. This is consistent with the public opinion work which suggests that people favour linking inheritance tax to educational spending over the Child Trust Fund (Lewis and White 2006).[8] In this case, the spending can be seen as an investment which is likely to help children mature into more creative and responsible adults. Moral intuitions about equal opportunity and responsible, pro-social behaviour can work together in a mutually reinforcing way.

Finally, we must ask: *Who* is to make the case for a reformed inheritance tax to help equalize life chances? As we noted in Chapter 1, it is unreasonable to place the burden of responsibility entirely on government. The popularization of the case against inheritance tax has been ably assisted in the UK by citizen-led organizations like the Taxpayers' Alliance. Our review of the estate tax repeal in the USA showed how important citizen-led campaigning was there too. There is a need, therefore, for a citizen-led defence of inheritance tax. A citizen-led, public campaign of defence is essential to create a climate of opinion in which government feels more able to take a principled stand in defence of the tax.

Probably such a citizen-led campaigning group would not be specifically concerned with the defence of inheritance tax. Rather, it would aim at campaigning in a more general way for a progressive tax system, mirroring the way that groups like the Taxpayers' Alliance are focused on a general agenda of tax cuts. This organization might be built up from existing groups which have an interest in creating a more balanced public debate about tax: trade unions, anti-poverty and children's welfare groups, Living Wage campaigns, and progressive church groups.

We hope that this short pamphlet can contribute to getting such an organization off the ground.

Conclusion

The pre-budget report of October 2007 was a profoundly depressing moment for those interested in fair taxation. The taxation of wealth transfers across the generations is a vital democratic principle, without which we cannot make good on the promise of equal opportunity. The pre-budget report offered no defence of this vital democratic principle. It was a moment of panic-driven surrender to a direct, unashamed attack on this principle.

Thankfully, this need not be the last word. The moral arguments for inheritance tax are compelling, the objections weak. We can make a powerful political case for a reformed inheritance tax as one item in a wider strategy to create a society in which citizens enjoy tolerably equal life chances. But the word 'citizen' here is instructive. The events of October 2007 reflect how vulnerable a social democratic government can be when it lacks the support of a strong, citizen-led, public campaign which broadly supports its values. Such a citizen-led, public campaign for fair taxation is what we urgently need. Tax politics – a progressive, social democratic tax politics – cannot be a politics of enlightened technocracy in which well-intentioned experts decide what is good *for* the people. It must be – it must become – a politics *of* the people.

Notes

Chapter 1

1 http://www.hmrc.gov.uk/stats/inheritance_tax/description-of-tax.pdf.

2 http://www.hmrc.gov.uk/stats/tax_receipts/table1-4.pdf.

3 http://www.hmrc.gov.uk/stats/tax_receipts/table1-2.pdf

Chapter 3

1 All too easily, talk of tax justice tacitly assumes the essential justice of the free market distribution of income and wealth and then asks how the pain or burden of taxation can be fairly extracted from people's pre-tax entitlements. It is, however, a mistake to regard the tax system as external to entitlement in this way. Principles of social justice, such as the principle of equality of opportunity, provide guidance as to how to design the tax system. When taxes are such as to satisfy these principles of social justice, people are entitled to what they get under the resulting tax system. Tax, set at a just level, helps to define entitlement rather than being an imposition on a pre-tax entitlement that is itself just. On this point we are indebted to Murphy and Nagel (2001).

2 For relevant theoretical and empirical work on how financial inheritance can affect opportunities for business formation, see Hoff (1998) and Blanchflower and Oswald (1998).

3 It is not a necessary truth that neutralizing inequality in financial inheritance will improve equality of opportunity. It depends on how inequality in financial inheritance is related to inequality in other kinds of inheritance. However, if inequality in financial inheritance is positively correlated with inequalities in other kinds of inheritance, such as in human capital, then reducing inequality in financial inheritances will improve overall equality of opportunity. The evidence presented in Chapter 2 on the class profile of financial inheritances suggests that this is the case.

4 Alf has more opportunity in the sense that he has a higher probability of getting any particular job in competition with Betty and Carl than in the world where they are able to use inheritances to gain a competitive edge over him.

Chapter 4

1 A further point is that we do not necessarily have to regard existing economic motivations as given. If we find that an inheritance tax does have an undesirable effect on work or saving, then we might see this as a reason for the state to try to cultivate a social ethos that would allow us to have inheritance tax, which is desirable on grounds of justice, without this affecting work or saving. For an excellent discussion of the importance of attending to ethocs in considering our response to incentives-based arguments for inequality, see Cohen (2000).

Chapter 5

1 http://petitions.pm.gov.uk/ihtcrusade/

2 http://news.bbc.co.uk/1/hi/uk_politics/5267836.stm

3 http://www.taxpayersalliance.com/

4 http://news.bbc.co.uk/1/hi/england/wiltshire/6174803.stm

5 http://news.bbc.co.uk/1/hi/uk_politics/5267836.stm

6 Recent details of the Irish Capital Acquisitions Tax can be found at http://www.revenue.ie/index.htm?/revguide/capitalacquisitionstax.htm

7 David Halpern (2007) has recently suggested encouraging parents to donate to their grandchildren or great-grandchildren rather than children as a possible route for reform. Halpern argues that while the intellectual case for inheritance tax is sound, it is not easy to win public support for this because it conflicts with a widely held emotional desire to leave to one's family. He says that this public hostility means that those interested in reducing wealth inequality should search for other types of policy. He proposes bequest trusts as one such policy. This would work with a popular wish to leave to one's family, but introduce a twist that would help reduce wealth inequality. Parents would establish trusts for their grandchildren or great-grandchildren. He notes that currently parents tend to bequeath to their children. He continues that the correlation between a parent's income and a child's income is typically close, but that this correlation falls the further one goes down the family tree. Halpern claims that as a result of this, encouraging people to leave their estate to their more distant descendants is powerfully redistributive, and this holds even after accounting for the tendency of the wealthy to mate with one another. We regard this as a very interesting proposal, worthy of serious further investigation, but we do not feel able to recommend it in the absence of further investigation to establish its effects under different assumptions.

8 It should be noted that this study also found that people were even more favourable to the proposal to link inheritance tax to spending on long-term care for the elderly.

Bibliography

Acheson, D. (1998), *Independent Inquiry into Inequalities in Health* (London: The Stationery Office), at http://www.archive.official-documents.co.uk/document/doh/ih/ih.htm.

Atkinson, A.B. (1972), *Unequal Shares: Wealth in Britain* (London: Penguin Press).

Becker, G. and Tomes, N. (1979), 'An equilibrium theory pf the distribtion of income and intergenerational mobility', *Journal of Political Economy* 87 (6), pp.1153-1189.

Blanchflower, D. and Oswald, A. (1998), 'What Makes an Entrepreneur?', *Journal of Labor Economics* 16, pp.26-60.

Bracewell-Milnes, B. (2002), *Euthanasia for Death Duties: Putting Inheritance Tax Out of Its Misery* (London: Institute of Economic Affairs).

Brighouse, H. and Swift, A., 'Legitimate Parental Partiality', forthcoming.

Castell, S. and Thompson, J. (2007), *Understanding Attitudes to Poverty in the UK. Getting the Public's Attention* (York: Joseph Rowntree Foundation), available at http://www.jrf.org.uk/bookshop/eBooks/2000-poverty-attitudes-uk.pdf.

Cohen, G.A. (2000), *If You're An Egalitarian, How Come You're So Rich?* (Cambridge, MA: Harvard University Press).

Commission on Life Chances and Child Poverty (2006), *Narrowing the Gap: the final report of the Fabian Commission on Life Chances and Child Poverty* (London: The Fabian Society).

Commission on Taxation and Citizenship (2000), *Paying for Progress: a New Politics of Tax for Public Spending* (London: The Fabian Society).

Darton, D., Hirsch, D. and Strelitz, J. (2003), *Tacking disadvantage: a 20-year enterprise* (York: Joseph Rowntree Foundation).

Ermisch, J., Francesconi, M. and Siedler, T. (2006), 'Intergenerational mobility and marital sorting', *Economic Journal* 116, pp.659-679.

Elster, J. (1986), 'Comments on Krouse and McPherson', *Ethics* 97, pp.146-153.

Finch, J. and Mason, J. (2000), *Passing On: Kinship and Inheritance in England* (London: Routledge).

Finch, J., Mason, J., Masson, J., Hayes, L. and Wallis, L. (1996), *Wills, Inheritance and Families* (Oxford: Oxford University Press).

Forrest, R. and Murie, A. (1989), 'Differential Accumulation: Wealth, Inheritance and Housing Policy Reconsidered', *Policy and Politics*, 19 (2), pp.109-118.

Forrest, R., Murie, A. and Williams, P. (1990), *Home Ownership* (London: Unwin Hyman).

Gale, W. and Perozek, M. (2001), 'Do Estate Taxes Reduce Saving?', in W. Gale, J. Hines and J. Slemrod, eds., *Rethinking Estate and Gift Taxation* (Washington, D.C.: Brookings Institute).

Gokhale, J., Kotlikoff, L., Sefton, J. and Weale, M. (2001), 'Simulating the transmission of wealth inequality via bequests', *Journal of Public Economics* 79, pp.93-128.

Graetz, M. and Shapiro, I. (2005), *Death by a Thousand Cuts: The Fight over Taxing Inherited Wealth* (Princeton: Princeton University Press).

Halpern, David (2007), 'Better bequests', *Prospect*, November 2007.

Hamnett, C. (1991), 'A nation of inheritors? Housing inheritance, wealth and inequality in Britain', *Journal of Social Policy* 20, pp.509-36.

Hamnett, C. (1997), 'Housing Wealth, Inheritance and Residential Care in

Britain', *Housing Finance,* 34, May.

Harbury, C. and Hitchens, D. (1979), *Inheritance and Wealth Inequality in Britain* (London: Allen and Unwin).

Hedges, A. and Bromley, C. (2001), *Public Attitudes Towards Taxation: the report of research conducted for the Fabian Commission on Taxation and Citizenship* (London: The Fabian Society).

Her Majesty's Revenue and Customs (2007), *Table 12.3, Inheritance Tax: estates notified for probate*, at http://www.hmrc.gov.uk/stats/inheritance_tax/07ir123.pdf.

Her Majesty's Treasury (2003), *Detailed Proposals for the Child Trust Fund* (London: The Stationery Office).

Her Majesty's Treasury, (2007), *Meeting the Aspirations of the British Public. The 2007 pre-budget report and comprehensive spending review,* Command paper 7227 (London: The Stationery Office).

Hills, J. (2004), *Inequality and the State* (Oxford: Oxford University Press).

Hoff, K. (1998), 'Market Failures and the Distribution of Wealth: A Perspective From the Economics of Information', in S. Bowles and H. Gintis, with E. Wright, ed., *Recasting Egalitarianism* (London, Verso), pp.332-357.

Holmans, A. (1991), 'Estimates of housing equity withdrawal by owner-occupiers in the United Kingdom 1970 to 1990', *Government Economic Service Working Paper* No. 116.

Holmans, A. (1997a), 'Housing and Inheritance Revisited', *Housing Finance* 33, February.

Holmans, A. (1997b), *Housing Inheritance: Current Trends and Future Prospects* (London: Council of Mortgage Lenders).

Holtz-Eakin, D. (1996), 'The Uneasy Empirical Case for Abolishing the Estate Tax', *Tax Law Review* 51, pp.495-515.

Hutton, W. (2007), 'The case for keeping inheritance tax', *The Observer,* October 7.

Inland Revenue (2003), *Inland Revenue Statistics 2003* (London: Inland

Revenue).

Laitner, J. (1979a), 'Household bequests, perfect explanations, and the national distribution of wealth', *Econometrica* 47 (5), pp.1175-1193.

Laitner, J. (1979b), 'Household bequest behaviour and the national distribution of wealth', *Review of Economic Studies* 46 (3), pp.467-483.

Lewis, M. and White, S. (2006), 'Inheritance tax: what do people think? Evidence from deliberative workshops', in Paxton, W., White, S. and Maxwell, D. (ed), *The Citizen's Stake: exploring the future of universal asset policies* (Bristol: Policy Press), 15-35.

McCaffery, E. (1994), 'The Political Liberal Case Against the Estate Tax', *Philosophy and Public Affairs* 23 (4), pp.281-312.

McClean, I. (2007), 'Opinion: 'Dead People Pay No Tax'', *The Observer*, Cash section, October 21, at http://observer.guardian.co.uk/cash/story/0,,2195881,00.html.

Menchik, P. (1979), 'Intergeneration transmission of inequality: an empirical study of wealth mobility', *Economica* 46, pp.349-362.

Miller, D. (2000), *Principles of Social Justice* (Cambridge, MA: Harvard University Press).

Murphy, L. and Nagel, T. (2001), *The Myth of Ownership* (Oxford: Oxford University Press).

Nissan, D. and Le Grand, J. (2000), *A Capital Idea: Start-up Grants for Young People* (London: The Fabian Society).

O'Neill, M. (2007), 'Death and Taxes', *New Statesman* on-line, October 8, at http://www.newstatesman.com/200710080002.
——— (2008), 'Death and Taxes', *Renewal* 15 (4).

Osborne, G. (2007), 'It's Time for Aspiration', at http://www.conservatives.com/tile.do?def=news.story.page&obj_id=139170.

Paine, T. (1987 [1797]), *Agrarian Justice*, in M. Foot and I. Kramnick, eds., *The Thomas Paine Reader* (Harmondsworth: Penguin), pp.471-489.

Patrick, R. and Jacobs, M. (2003), *Wealth's Fair Measure: The Reform of*

Inheritance Tax (London: Fabian Society).

Paxton, W. (2002), *Wealth distribution: the evidence* (London: ippr).

Paxton, W. and White, S. with Maxwell, D. (2006), *The Citizen's Stake: Exploring the Future of Universal Asset Policies* (Bristol: Policy Press).

Prabhakar, R. (2008a), 'Wealth Taxes: Stories, Metaphors and Public Attitudes', *Political Quarterly*, forthcoming.

Prabhakar, R. (2008b), *The Assets Agenda: principles and policy* (Basingstoke: Palgrave).

Rawls, J. (1999 [1971]), *A Theory of Justice: Revised Edition* (Cambridge, MA: Harvard University Press).

Rowlingson, K. (2008), 'Is the Death of Inheritance Tax Inevitable? Lessons from America', *Political Quarterly*, forthcoming.

Rowlingson, K. and McKay, S. (2005), *Attitudes to Inheritance in Britain* (Bristol: Policy Press).
The *Findings* is downloadable from: http://www.jrf.org.uk/knowledge/findings/socialpolicy/0385.asp.
The full report is downloadable from:
http://www.jrf.org.uk/bookshop/eBooks/1861347707.pdf.

Runciman, D. (2005), 'Tax Breaks for Rich Murderers', *London Review of Books* 27 (11), at http://www.lrb.co.uk/v27/n11/runc01_.html.

Sandford, C. (1971), *Taxing Personal Wealth* (London: Allen and Unwin).
———, and Willis, J.R.M., Ironside, D.J. (1973), *An Accessions Tax: A Study of the Desirability and Feasibility of Replacing the United Kingdom Estate Duty with a Cumulative Tax on Recipients of Gifts and Inheritances* (London: Institute for Fiscal Studies).

Saunders, P. (1986), 'Comment on Dunleavy and Preteceille', *Society and Space* 4, pp.155-163.

Stiglitz, J (1969), 'Distribution of Wealth among individuals' *Econometrica* 37 (3), pp. 382-397.

Szydlik, M (2004), 'Inheritance and Inequality: Theoretical Reasoning and Empirical Evidence, *European Sociological Review,* Vol 20, No 1, pp. 31-45.

Tait, A. (1967), *The Taxation of Personal Wealth* (Chicago, University of Illinois Press).

Tawney, R. H. (1964 [1931]), *Equality* (London: Allen and Unwin).

Thompson, M. (2007), *The Politics of Inequality: A Political History of the Idea of Economic Inequality in America* (New York: Columbia University Press).

Toynbee, P. (2007), 'Now the crisis is over, ditch the muzzle of consensus', *The Guardian*, October 9.

Wedgwood, J (1939), *The Economics of Inheritance,* (London: Pelican Books)

White, S. (2006), *Equality* (Cambridge: Polity).

Wilhelm, M (1996) 'Bequest behaviour and the effect of heirs' earnings: testing the altruistic model of bequests' *American Economic Review,* vol 86, pp. 874-92.

Wilhelm, M (1997), 'Inheritance, steady-state consumption inequality and the lifetime earnings process', *Manchester School of Economic and Social Studies,* 65 (4) pp. 466-476.

Wolff, E. (1996), 'Commentary', *Tax Law Review* 51, pp.517-521.

Wolff, E (2002), 'Inheritances and Wealth Inequality, 1989-1998' *American Economics Association Papers and Proceedings,* Bequests, Saving and Wealth Inequality, vol 92, 2, pp. 260-264.

Discussion Guide: Inheritance Tax

Defending Inheritance Tax

How to Defend Inheritance Tax
by Rajiv Prabhakar, Karen Rowlingson and Stuart White

How to use this Discussion Guide

The guide can be used in various ways by Fabian Local Societies, local political party meetings and trade union branches, student societies, NGOs and other groups.

- You might hold a discussion among local members or invite a guest speaker – for example, an MP, academic or local practioner to lead a group discussion.
- Four different key themes are suggested. You might choose to spend 15 – 20 minutes on each area, or decide to focus the whole discussion on one of the issues for a more detailed discussion.

A discussion could address some or all of the following questions:

1. Principles

Finding ways to reconnect arguments about tax to a social justice agenda is one of the concerns underpinning this pamphlet. Drawing on evidence from the campaign to repeal inheritance taxes in America, the authors argue that defenders of inheritance must draw on moral, as well as pragmatic, arguments to defend inheritance tax.

- In your experience, what are some of the most common objections to inheritance tax?
- And what are the most effective counter arguments? Which moral arguments are likely to have the most impact?

2. Policy

The authors argue that reforming inheritance by replacing it with a capital receipts tax would help to tackle many of the objections to inheritance tax.

- Could changing the form of tax remove some of the objections to inheritance tax, and is a capital receipts tax the best model?

3. Politics

At present, very few people are prepared to make the case for inheritance tax. The pamphlet argues that if inheritance tax is to resist repeal, there will need to be a citizen led campaign to support it.

- How could progressive groups such as anti-poverty NGOs, trade unions and political parties work together to make the case for inheritance tax?
- What would an effective campaign look like, and what might some of its key messages be?

Please let us know what you think

Whatever view you take of the issues, we would very much like to hear about your discussion. Please send us a summary of your debate (perhaps 300 words) to debate@fabians.org.uk. We would like to publish comments alongside the discussion guide at www.fabians.org.uk and in the Fabian Review.

The Fabian Review, Winter 2007

The Fabian Review, Autumn 2007

The Fabian Review, Summer 2007

How progressive politics can tackle political extremism

The rise of extremists – such as the British National Party – is one of the most worrying trends of recent times. With ever more candidates, increased media attention and a rising number of votes, the BNP seems to be here to stay. They have capitalised on the disengagement, disenfranchisement and fear that many votes in more deprived communities feel.

Stopping the Far Right argues that anyone involved in the Labour Party, trade unions and the wider progressive movement should join the response to this challenge. Through a detailed look at the recent history of British far right politics and a careful consideration of the current situation, the authors hope to engage all those who are ideologically opposed to the BNP. Stopping the Far Right aims to act as a practical tool for anyone who is engaged in this argument.

How party politics must change to build a progressive society

Reconnecting people to politics is the issue of the moment. Alongside public scrutiny of our constitutional settlement, and the rights and responsibilities of citizenship, political renewal must also involve thinking again about how parties can contribute to strengthening democracy.

In **Facing Out**, the authors reject the idea that political parties are a relic of the past, and show how populist frustration with party politics can often demonstrate a refusal to confront the compromises and trade-offs that remain the essence of democracy. Yet parties will need to change to remain relevant and to respond to the transformations in society that are threatening all political parties.

The central question must be how Labour can remain at the forefront of campaigning for progressive change.

Special offer: join the Fabians for just £9.95 and get this book free.

'The Fabians ask the most difficult questions, pushing Labour to make a bold, progressive case on taxation and the abolition of child poverty.' – **Polly Toynbee**

How can we make poverty history at home?

One in five children still grows up in poverty in Britain. Yet all the political parties now claim to care about 'social justice'. This report sets a litmus test by which Brown, Cameron and Campbell must be judged.

'**Narrowing the Gap**' is the final report of the Fabian Commission on Life Chances and Child Poverty, chaired by Lord Victor Adebowale. The Fabian Society is the only think tank with members. Join us and help us put poverty and equality at the centre of the political agenda.

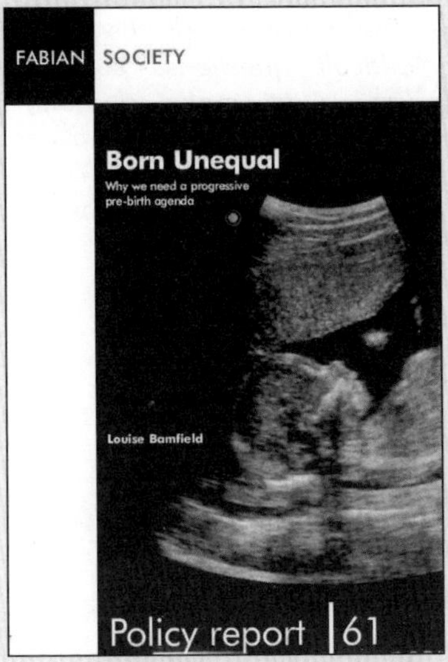

Why we need a progressive pre-birth agenda

In Britain, by the time a baby is born, its chances of living a healthy, fulfilling life are already decided. Building on 'Narrowing the Gap', **Louise Bamfield** examines the reasons for inequalities at birth and explores the ways in which government can act to support maternal and foetal health.

While the Government has begun to recognise the need for a pre-birth policy, it has yet to make a progressive case for it. This policy report argues that the Government's attack on child poverty and inequality risks being undermined by the punitive public narrative that has emerged in recent years around anti-social behaviour and the politics of 'respect'. If action to tackle inequalities before birth is to gain the support necessary carry it forward, the Government must make the case for a progressive pre-birth agenda.

How to break the hospitals' grip on the NHS

In this Fabian pamphlet, **Dr Howard Stoate MP** says that the Government's future NHS vision will fail if they cannot find a compelling public argument which can win locally against the 'save the hospital' brigade.

Challenging the Citadel: Breaking the hospitals' grip on the NHS sees health select committee member Dr Stoate and Bryan Jones argue that the NHS is far too focused on the hospital as an institution.

The new NHS should be about public health and health prevention, and if the dominance of the hospitals continues we will find ourselves unable to make substantial improvements in health outcomes, and the NHS will be ill-equipped to cope with the pressures it will face in the 21st century.

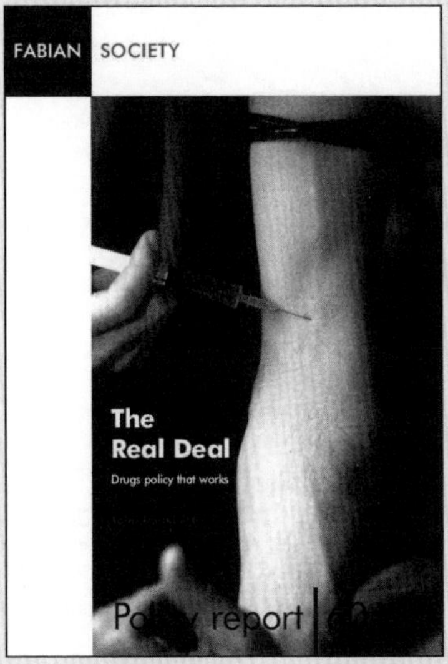

The Real Deal: a drugs policy that works

In the Fabian policy report The **Real Deal: Drugs policy that works** the senior backbencher **John Mann MP** set out the case for a radical overhaul of UK drugs policy.

Mann argues for a new approach to drugs classification, and for compulsory drugs treatment for addicts involved in crime. He says that "coercion should be recognised as not only legitimate but necessary to get users off chronically addictive drugs such as heroin" and says that concerns about civil liberties are misplaced because "free choice" is meaningless for serious addicts.

The report's recommendations seek to address the links between drug addiction and crime, based on work done in John Mann's Bassetlaw constituency where the decision to treat drug use as a medical problem massively reduced drug-related crime.

Will the Make Poverty History generation lose its commitment?

Britain came a long way between Live Aid in 1985 and Live 8 in 2005. The Fabian pamphlet **2025: What next for the Make Poverty History generation?**, edited by **Tom Hampson**, asks what the next twenty years could hold.

What positive vision for 2025 is needed to keep the British public mobilised? Despite Live 8, individualism is now stronger than community.

For the first time since 1994, according to our Henley data, a majority of people says that looking after ourselves is more important to quality of life than looking after our communities.

Hilary Benn, Robert Cooper, Tom Hampson, Clare Short and Vandana Shiva set out their own visions of global change and the politics needed to make them a reality.

JOIN THE FABIANS TODAY

Join us and receive two Fabian Reviews, plus our award-winning equality report, 'Narrowing the Gap'

I'd like to become a Fabian for just £9.95

I understand that should at any time during my six-month introductory membership period I wish to cancel, I will receive a refund and keep all publications received without obligation. After six months I understand my membership will revert to the annual rate as published in *Fabian Review*, currently £31 (ordinary) or £14 (unwaged).

Name | Date of birth

Address

Postcode

Email

Telephone

Instruction to Bank Originator's ID: 971666

DIRECT Debit

Bank/building society name

Address

Postcode

Acct holder(s)

Acct no. | Sort code

I instruct you to pay direct debits from my account at the request of the Fabian Society. The instruction is subject to the safeguards of the Direct Debit Guarantee.

Signature | Date

Return to:
Fabian Society Membership
FREEPOST SW 1570
11 Dartmouth Street
London
SW1H 9BN